OXFORD

UNIVERSITY PRESS

How to Draw Yourself

Sharon Holt

You can draw a picture of yourself.

2

What you will need:

a mirror

a pencil

paper

crayons

3

What to do:
1. Look in a mirror.

4

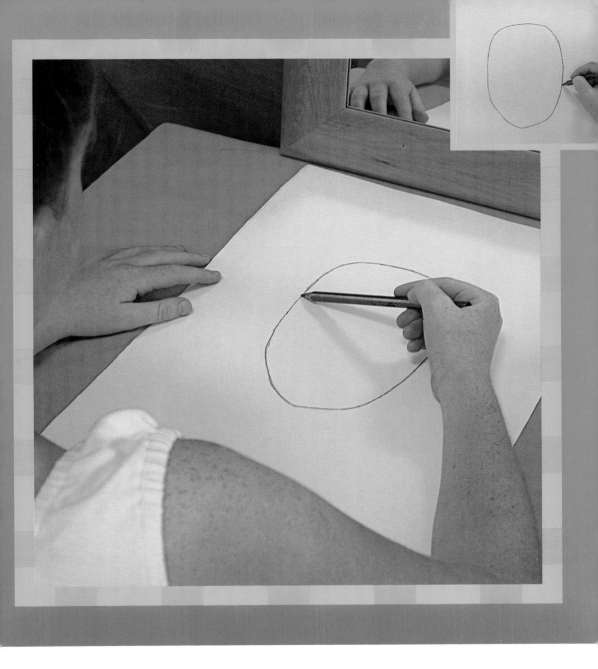

2. Draw a big egg shape.

3. Look at the picture.
4. Draw a line across the egg.

6

5. Draw your eyes and
your ears on the line.

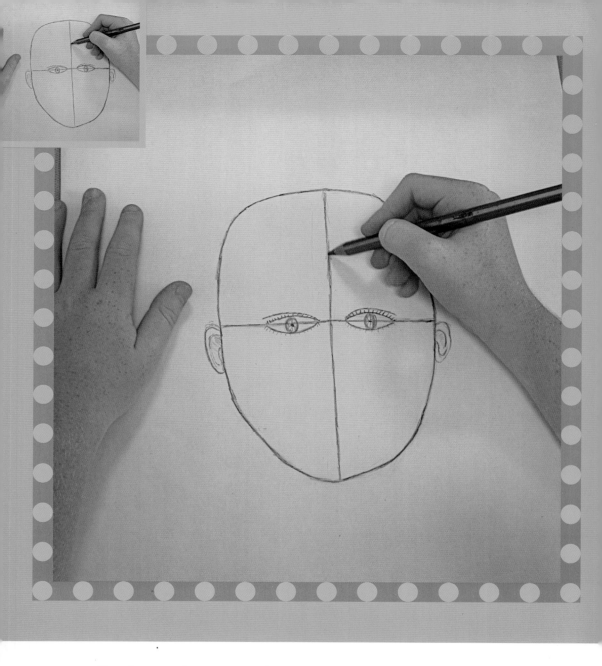

6. Look at the picture.

7. Draw a line down the egg.

8. Draw your nose on the line.

9. Draw two more lines across the egg.

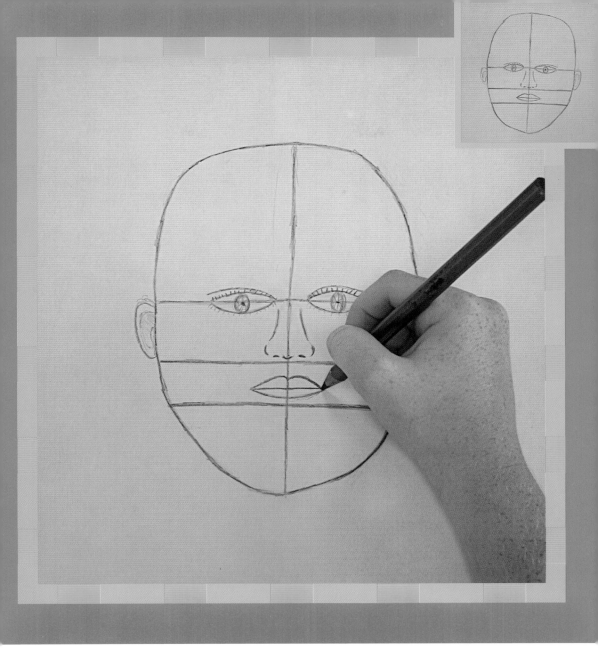

10. Draw your mouth.

11. Look in the mirror.
12. Look at your hair.

12

13. Draw your hair on your picture.

13

14. Colour in your picture.

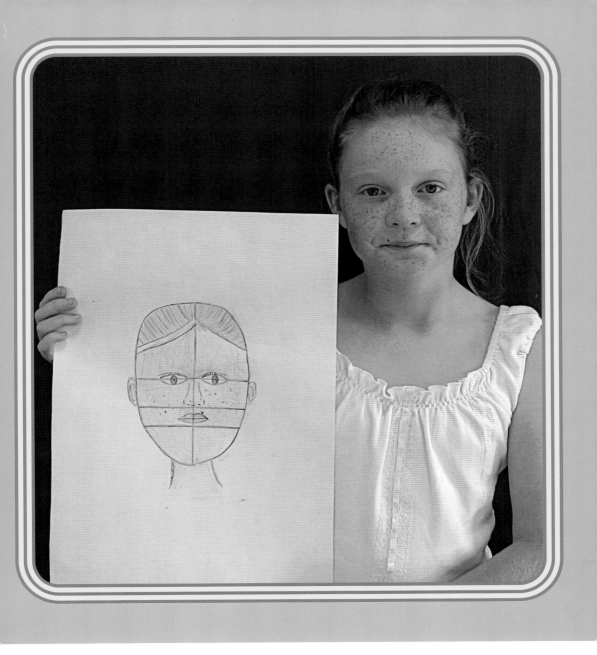

Now you have a picture
of yourself.

How to Draw Yourself

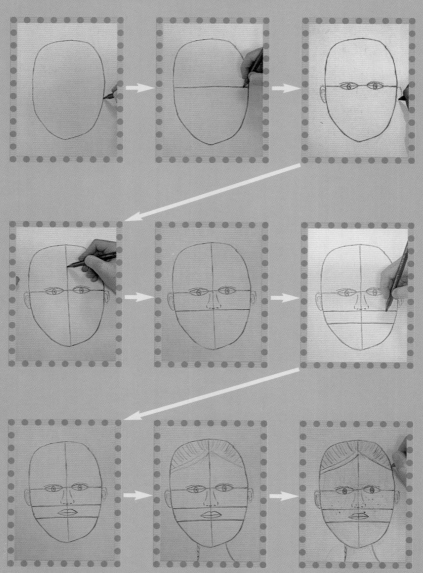